Catherine Bruzzone and Louise Millar

Illustrations by Clare Beaton

French adviser: Marie-Thérèse Bougard

KT-198-299

My First 100 French Words

la jupe
la shoop
skirt

le pyjama
*ler peeshah-**mah***
pyjamas

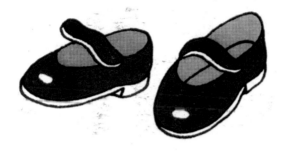

les chaussures
*leh showss-**yoor***
shoes

le manteau
*ler mon**to***
coat

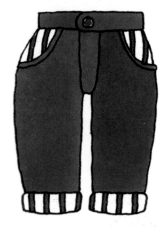

le pantalon
*ler ponta-**loh***
trousers

la robe
la rob
dress

4

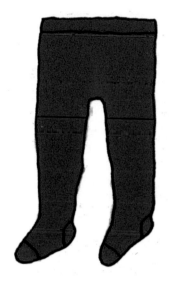

les collants
leh koll-oh
tights

le chapeau
ler shapo
hat

Les vêtements
leh vetmoh

le tee-shirt
ler tee-shirt
T-shirt

les bottes
leh bot
boots

les chaussettes
*leh show-**set***
socks

le maillot de bain
*ler my-**o** der **bah***
swimming costume

le ballon
*ler bah-**loh***
ball

les crayons de couleur
*leh cray-**oh** der cool-**err***
crayons

la poupée
*la poo-**peh***
doll

le tambour
*ler tom**boor***
drum

les cubes
leh kube
blocks

le tricycle
*ler tree-**see**-kl'*
tricycle

le nounours
*ler noo-**noorss***
teddy bear

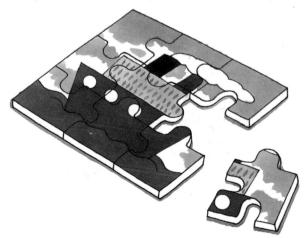

le puzzle
ler poozl'
puzzle

la pomme
la pom
apple

le pain
ler pah
bread

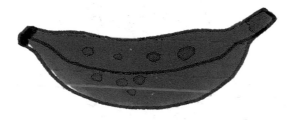

la banane
*la ban-**an***
banana

l'œuf
lerf
egg

le fromage
*ler from**aj***
cheese

la carotte
*la kah-**rot***
carrot

le chocolat
*ler shoko**lah***
chocolate

l'eau
loh
water

la tomate
*la to-**mat***
tomato

les pâtes
leh pat
pasta

l'orange
*lo**ronsh***
orange

le sandwich
*ler sond**weech***
sandwich

La fête

la fet

les biscuits
*leh beesk-**wee***
biscuits

le gâteau
*ler gat**oh***
cake

la boisson
*la bwas**soh***
drink

le ballon
*ler bah-**loh***
balloon

le chapeau de fête
ler shapo der fet
party hat

le cadeau
ler kad-o
present

Party

la glace
la glas
ice-cream

les cupcakes
leh kop-kek
cupcakes

la serviette
la sairvee-et
towel

le shampooing
*ler shom-**pwang***
shampoo

22

la brosse à dents
*la bross ah **doh***
toothbrush

le savon
*ler sa**voh***
soap

la cuillère
*la kwee-**yair***
spoon

la casserole
*la kasse**rol***
saucepan

24

le bol
ler bol
bowl

le tablier
ler tab-lee-eh
apron

le bac à sable
ler bak ah sabl'
sandpit

la balançoire
*la balon-**swah***
swing

le toboggan
*ler to-bog-**oh***
slide

le banc
ler bonk
bench

le chat
ler shah
cat

le chien
*ler shee-**yah***
dog

l'oiseau
*lwaz-**oh***
bird

la souris
*la soo-**ree***
mouse

la vache
la vash
COW

la chèvre
la shevr
goat

le lapin
*ler lah-**pah***
rabbit

le mouton
*ler moo-**toh***
sheep

la poule
la pool
chicken

le cheval
ler sh-val
horse

le cochon
*ler koh-**shoh***
pig

le canard
*ler kan-**ar***
duck

33

la voiture
*la vwot-**yoor***
car

le bateau
*ler bat**o***
boat

l'avion
*lavee-**on***
aeroplane

la moto
*la moh-**to***
motorbike

la bicyclette
*la beesee-**klet***
bicycle

l'autobus
*low-toh-**boos***
bus

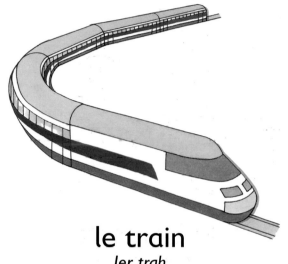

le train
ler trah
train

le tracteur
*ler trak-**ter***
tractor

le nuage
*ler noo-**ah**-sh*
cloud

la pluie
la plwee
rain

le parapluie
*ler pah-rah-**plwee***
umbrella

l'arc-en-ciel
*larkon-see-**ell***
rainbow

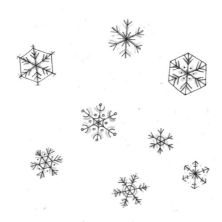

la neige
la nair'sh
snow

l'orage
*lor-**ah**-sh*
storm

le bonhomme de neige
*ler bon**om** der nair'sh*
snowman

le soleil
*ler sol-**ay***
sun

Les couleurs

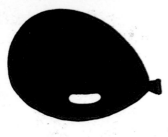

rouge
rooshj
red

bleu/bleue
bl'/bl'
blue

jaune
shown
yellow

rose
roz
pink

vert/verte
vair/vairt
green

noir/noire
nwah/nwah
black

orange
oranshj
orange

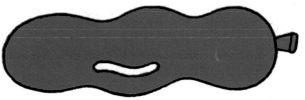

violet/violette
*veeoh-**leh**/veeoh-**let***
purple

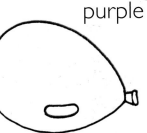

blanc/blanche
bloh/blonsh
white

marron
*mah-**roh***
brown

Les nombres

leh nombr'

1 un
ahn
one

2 deux
der
two

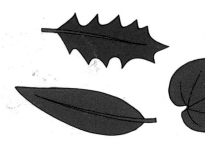

3 trois
trwah
three

4 quatre
katr'
four

5 cinq
sank
five

44

Numbers

6 six
seess
six

7 sept
set
seven

8 huit
weet
eight

9 neuf
nerf
nine

10 dix
deess
ten

Vocabulaire

*voh-kab-oo-**lair***

French/français – English/anglais
*fron-**seh***   *on-**gleh***

les animaux animals
l'arc-en-ciel rainbow
l'autobus bus
l'avion aeroplane
le bac à sable sandpit
la balançoire swing
le ballon ball; balloon
la banane banana
le banc bench
le bateau boat
la bicyclette bicycle
les biscuits biscuits
blanc/blanche white
bleu/bleue blue
la boisson drink
le bol bowl
le bonhomme de neige snowman
les bottes boots
la brosse à dents toothbrush
le cadeau present
le canard duck
la carotte carrot
la casserole saucepan
le chapeau hat
le chapeau de fête party hat
le chat cat
les chaussettes socks
les chaussures shoes
le cheval horse
la chèvre goat
le chien dog
le chocolat chocolate
cinq five
le cochon pig
les collants tights
les couleurs colours
les crayons de couleur crayons

les cubes blocks
la cuillère spoon
la cuisine cooking
les cupcakes cupcakes
deux two
dix ten
l'eau water
la fête party
le fromage cheese
le gâteau cake
la glace ice-cream
l'heure du bain bathtime
huit eight
jaune yellow
les jouets toys
la jupe skirt
le lapin rabbit
le maillot de bain swimming costume
le manteau coat
marron brown
le moto motorbike
le mouton sheep
la neige snow
neuf nine
noir/noire black
les nombres numbers
le nounours teddy bear
la nourriture food
le nuage cloud
l'œuf egg
l'oiseau bird
l'orage storm
orange orange (colour)
l'orange orange (fruit)
le pain bread
le pantalon trousers

la parapluie umbrella
les pâtes pasta
la pluie rain
la pomme apple
la poule chicken
la poupée doll
le puzzle puzzle
le pyjama pyjamas
quatre four
la robe dress
rose pink
rouge red
le sandwich sandwich
le savon soap
sept seven
la serviette towel
le shampooing shampoo
six six
le soleil sun
la souris mouse
le tablier apron
le tambour drum
le tee-shirt T-shirt
le temps weather
le terrain de jeux playground
le toboggan slide
la tomate tomato
le tracteur tractor
le train train
le transport transport
le tricycle tricycle
trois three
un one
la vache cow
vert/verte green
les vêtements clothes
violet/violette purple
la voiture car

Word list

aeroplane l'avion
animals les animaux
apple la pomme
apron le tablier
ball le ballon
balloon le ballon
banana la banane
bathtime
  l'heure du bain
bench le banc
bicycle la bicyclette
bird l'oiseau
biscuits les biscuits
black noir/noire
blocks les cubes
blue bleu/bleue
boat le bateau
boots les bottes
bowl le bol
bread le pain
brown marron
bus l'autobus
cake le gâteau
car la voiture
carrot la carotte
cat le chat
cheese le fromage
chicken la poule
chocolate le chocolat
clothes les vêtements
cloud le nuage
coat le manteau
colours les couleurs
cooking la cuisine
cow la vache
crayons
  les crayons de couleur
cupcakes les cupcakes
dog le chien
doll la poupée
dress la robe

drink la boisson
drum le tambour
duck le canard
egg l'œuf
eight huit
five cinq
food la nourriture
four quatre
goat la chèvre
green vert/verte
hat le chapeau
horse le cheval
ice-cream la glace
motorbike la moto
mouse la souris
nine neuf
numbers les nombres
one un
orange (colour)
  orange
orange (fruit)
  l'orange
party la fête
party hat
  le chapeau de fête
pasta les pâtes
pig le cochon
pink rose
playground
  le terrain de jeux
present le cadeau
purple violet/violette
puzzle le puzzle
pyjamas le pyjama
rabbit le lapin
rain la pluie
rainbow l'arc-en-ciel
red rouge
sandpit le bac à sable
sandwich le sandwich
saucepan la casserole

seven sept
shampoo
  le shampooing
sheep le mouton
shoes les chaussures
six six
skirt la jupe
slide le toboggan
snow la neige
snowman
  le bonhomme de neige
soap le savon
socks les chaussettes
spoon la cuillère
storm l'orage
sun le soleil
swimming costume
  le maillot de bain
swing la balançoire
teddy bear le nounours
ten dix
three trois
tights les collants
tomato la tomate
toothbrush
  la brosse à dents
towel la serviette
toys les jouets
tractor le tracteur
train le train
transport le transport
tricycle le tricycle
trousers le pantalon
T-shirt le tee-shirt
two deux
umbrella le parapluie
water l'eau
weather le temps
white blanc/blanche
yellow jaune

© b small publishing ltd. 2012

The Book Shed, 36 Leyborne Park, Kew,
Richmond, Surrey, TW9 3HA

www.bsmall.co.uk

www.facebook.co.uk/bsmallpublishing

www.twitter.com/bsmallbear

ISBN: 978-1-908164-20-9

1 2 3 4 5

Editorial: Catherine Bruzzone and Louise Millar

Design: Louise Millar

Production: Madeleine Ehm

French adviser: Marie-Thérèse Bougard

Printed in China by WKT Co. Ltd.

British Library Cataloguing-in-Publication Data.
A catalogue record for this book
is available from the British Library.